Night Owl

Poems to read under the stars

A.D. France

BookLeaf Publishing

India | USA | UK

Made with ❤ on the BookLeaf Publishing Platform
www.bookleafpub.in
www.bookleafpub.com

Dedication

To all night owls and early birds

Preface

Read as you sit beneath the stars— always in the sky whether or not we can see them.

A.D. France

Acknowledgements

To my husband, parents, friends, and family:
I am a compilation of all the love you've shown

The Expedition

Decided on a Sunday, brushing my teeth in the morning
Casually obsessive, thinking
I'm writing things down
Cause we're floating in space
Celestially bound to craving meaning

Stayed up all night, rushing to find the words
Wrote every last thing, took from dawn to dusk
Expedition Eject These Thoughts From My Brain
An earthling's pursuit of fulfillment

How to travel for free

I slay dragons on a parachute in my new favorite book
In another, catch bad guys in dusty cowboy boots
Sipping tea on a dock, Pacific Northwest
Or saving someone's grandson in Vietnam

I'm looking at stars, floating at sea
This ocean has no monsters, that's how it's written to be
I'm a star on a stage or a witch in the woods
I've had all kinds imaginable of strange childhoods
I'm a rich woman that's lonely, traveling to find herself
Learning money can't buy happiness, in and of itself

I'm a hero in the morning
By evening, the villain
Or in London 1950, just a paperboy, delivering
I can embark on adventure or live a slow life, mundane
Travel Thailand by train, find and sign Kurt Cobain
Live alone in a palace, a queen in disdain
As she slowly learns how to friendships maintain

I can try different lives, depends on the week
I can be loud and brave or a wallflower, meek
I can choose the company that I want to keep

Collecting perspective with each chapter I read
This is how to travel for free

Wondering wanderers

Addicted to longing, to learning, and yearning
Admit it, we're all doing it, while the world keeps on turning
Going to Japan, Amsterdam, the bar down the street
Certain the answer is someone we could meet
Inspecting the globe, cyberspace, every book
Scouring each building and crevice and nook
Giving all our years and money to the quest
Go back two spaces if you end up depressed
Are we not all on the search for transcendence?
Weighing benefits and drawbacks of independent codependence?

The guide and the guided

He lays with the ants in the grass, no blanket
To hear the secrets they whisper and tell
To look at the trees, at the birds, the rain
If he looks long enough, they reveal what matters
The calm is lush, green, and everywhere
He's human, so he doesn't notice
He just has so much to worry about
But the trees and the rain and the green--- they know
So he lays with the ants to learn wisdom they show

Window weather

A beautiful sound—
Or lack thereof, when it touches the ground
Compels us to stop for a moment, take a look all around
A to-do list can wait when outside is sparkling

Theatrics aside, it's intensely exciting
When the sky turns white, not a cloud in sight, and we
know what comes next
Popcorn and Pepsi
Permission to rest
Simply that simple, the best

We open the blinds, fall asleep to the peace
Complain in the morning cause the neighbor shoveled
first
And now we have an excuse, we can't make it to the
thing
The snow said last night, *you can live just for living*

Your essence

We will all tell you how you look is entrancing
It's compelling to appease, we're relentlessly demanding
We think we're looking at you, we don't know we're not
What we want is to *see* you
But there's a lie we all bought

Halloween twenty-thirteen

I used to write about you in my diary
Hot summer days, humid and quiet
Thirteen, concerned, and didn't know your face
Fated to meet you, impatient with the wait
Just one of those things, the wise ways of life
I didn't know then in '24 I'd know why

Fast forward some years, on an October night
We both decided, not knowing quite why
I'm going to Hangar, and out the door we fly
And then we arrive. Thank you, *you're here!*
But sounded more, *What's your name?* Or some version
of that

Actually meant: *You look so familiar, I'll love you one
day*
Already did, since like twenty oh eight
Just didn't know your face and didn't want to wait
What took you so long, *come on, let's get married!*

The greatest adventure

I am from Italy, Spain
From the moon, the rain

I live in America, with politicians and artists
Been straddling cultures, big to imagine it

Here in the winter it snows in December
Midwest from Rio, the greatest adventure

To find beauty here, and then find it there
To spread dreams and watch them grow just about
anywhere

To make the world home
To follow those dreams
Constellation of cultures, a beautiful thing

Love is her favorite thing

Super Crazy Daisy Girl, Snow Feet, Little Pokemon
Princess Queen of the Bubblegum Kingdom
Protector of the Realm of our humble abode
Communicates in love and kisses and walks
And whipped cream with a tiny milk bone
Her least favorite thing: when the mailmen come
But the worst of the worst is being alone
Counting the seconds till we come back home

Human nature

Looking at the sky isn't enough
They have to paint it, photograph it, wrap it up, and drag
it home
They have to tie themselves together with it
Keep it from slipping through their fingers
They have to remember it, can't afford to forget

They look and don't see
They look again
Ah, now they see
They keep looking, stare it
They sit still, get quiet

They form a memory, they hold it tight, they feed it to
their souls
They try to remember, can't afford to forget:
What they won't take is the gold

I Choose the Bear

Look around, count the exits, code words for the kids,
did you share your location?
Keys in your fingers, lights on if not home, stay out of
big crowds, can't go alone
Pepper spray, don't stay out late, can I even throw a
punch?
No, I'm not going, changed my mind...
I just... have like... a hunch...
Did you see on the news? Still can't believe it, how scary
some people can be
Awake and aware, a burden to be when we really just
want to be free

Girl power

She cut me off! Didn't she see it?!
How can a driver be such an idiot??
I spent the next 20 thinking things that I'd say
If she'd roll down her window and hear me in rage
I finally pass her, show her my finger
And secretly hope it will ruin her day

And just when I think I came out the winner
She catches up, honks, and the air becomes thinner
I get a good look and I'm so disappointed
This girl thinks she's right, and she got what she wanted!

Think quick, should I follow her? Tell her my mind?
I didn't of course, only to my surprise
She pulls into the same garage I am going
I almost lost track, the event starts in 30

She steps out the car and looks like a goddess
Arrived at the same show, the craziest odds and...
We look at each other and all conflict lifts
We're both in hot pink, ready for Taylor Swift

We get in a hug and the past is the past
The beauty of girlhood, a bond happens fast

The moon is pretty but there's no water

"They're cutting trees down for money in pockets!"
Same day but later, building a rocket

The people shouted, *"the planet is dying!"*
And doctors and books called it textbook anxiety
But no pill could change it---
The panthers and pandas were really in danger

So the people, exhausted, took a deep breath
With their time and their minds, kept trying their best
Preached and pleaded *"live and let live!"*
And the story continued
The rest is the rest

Midnight Owl

15

The night owl hoots
Maybe I should go to sleep
But like magic, someone else is listening to the radio too
Different scenery, same frequency
Late night dreamers and ruminators
Who are out there like me, like you
Who wonder who hears the night owl hoot

Survival of the fittest

Imagine killing a spider halfway to her babies
Under a gorgeous blue sky, take a life, justify
Unaliving a fly while she's trying to fly
Live and let die, unless inconvenient
Unless there's a sound you strongly dislike
Disregard her objective: to only survive
Consider she's sentient and using her senses
Wonder what the fate of such an offense is

Imagine a world invaded by aliens
They're bigger and faster and aiming to claim us
They poison and squash us and trap us in glue
Like the small little mouse you just had to subdue
Only then understand: smaller life, just as grand

Infinite suns

Wake up outside on the right side of life
In a hammock, like clockwork, wake up with the suns
Take note how gratitude multiplies by the tons

Dance, sing, sit in the rain
Watch the sky fall and get back up again
Talk about gods, about soup, about nothing
Listen to nature, the song of her humming
Watch the plants grow, time stops passing by
See how it stops, turns around, waves goodbye

Forget about shoes, about clocks, about time
Know it is infinite, so wake up outside

Happily ever after

Once upon a time there was a boy and a girl
One liked the other, but wasn't loved back
Intermittent, inconsistent, and lacking commitment
But simple and summer and fun in the sun
For like two or three weeks, maybe six months
Just laughing and talking and playing and parties
And then they part ways, and there's no need for sorries
No really big lessons, maybe a couple of small ones
They knew it would end, not if, but when time comes
Just kids, can you blame them?
Heads in the clouds
But then one meets someone, and three is a crowd
They said their goodbyes and didn't look back
And that is the end, no one had to attack

Puzzle pieces

19

Resist the temptation to try to fit in
Impossible anyway, a game no one wins

You'll fit where you're meant
Bumpy ride along the way
The reward, being you, makes that perfectly okay

Alley cat

From rooftop to rooftop he strides slow with pride
Eyes on the sleeping city that happens to be his
Full moon in the sky and its light as his guide
Youngest thing he knows is the night of tonight

He strolls all around, does not make a sound
Some even say he is quiet as a mouse
Who was never his enemy, that was all pretend
When no one's looking, they're pretty good friends

One night in particular, he saw a girl, she seemed familiar
Followed her home and then needed a nap
Woke up on her doormat... curiosity and the cat

With a warm bowl of milk, that's how he was lured
She wanted to love him, her intentions were pure
And inside was amazing, endless pillows to himself
Warm milk at his command, whatever he wanted from the shelf

But he sat by the window as the next night came alive
The smell of the bistros, soft jazz in the distance
He could hear, taste, and smell it

He had to go live it

He left her a note with his small little nose
Heart shaped in the window, then took off to the
shadows
Don't worry about me, I'll always come back
But I was born to be wild, I'm the alliest cat

Reflection and deflection

22

I blame you, you, and you for all of my problems
Unraveling and raveling while pretending to solve 'em
Cover them up with a joke, something witty
Ghosting accountability from city to city

Curtains

Thanks for coming, the end
I'll never write a thought again
Should've seen me two a.m.
Wide awake thinking--- *I could, maybe should buy a*
shredder

Instead remembered a silly thing, a meme
Something like,
'Sharknado was somebody's dream so don't be scared
girl, say your thing'
I was just trying to fall asleep
Sometimes courage knocks like this
Tragically easy to miss or dismiss

But then: they can, and I can, we all can and should
Feed the fire, art's the wood
It's also the glue so we don't fall apart
Interchangeable with life
Till the end, since the start